Travel THE Highways OF Advent

Travel THE Highways OF Advent

An Advent Study for Adults

STAN PURDUM

Abingdon Press

Nashville

TRAVEL THE HIGHWAYS OF ADVENT
AN ADVENT STUDY FOR ADULTS
Copyright © 2014 by Abingdon Press

This book is printed on acid-free paper.

Library of Congress Cataloging-in-Publication Data

Purdum, Stan, 1945-
    Travel the highways of Advent : an Advent study for adults / Stan Purdum.
        pages cm
    ISBN 978-1-4267-8597-9 (book-pbk., adhesive perfect binding : alk. paper) 1. Advent--Prayers and devotions. 2. Bible--Devotional use. I. Title.
    BV40.P87 2014
    242'.332--dc23
                                                    2014022540

14 15 16 17 18 19 20 21 22 23—10 9 8 7 6 5 4 3 2 1
MANUFACTURED IN THE UNITED STATES OF AMERICA

Contents

Introduction 7

First Week of Advent
The Straightened and Leveled Highway 11

Second Week of Advent
The Highway of Reversal 27

Third Week of Advent
The Highway In Between 43

Fourth Week of Advent
The Highway of Enthusiasm 61

Christmas
The Highway of Merriment 77

Introduction

Travel the Highways of Advent

Do you know what the problem with Advent hymns is? Nobody wants to sing them. At least that was true in every church I pastored. For the service on the first Sunday of Advent, I'd select such hymns as "O Come, O Come, Emmanuel" or "Come, Thou Long-Expected Jesus," and folks would tolerate them; but if on the second Sunday, I used more Advent hymns, someone would stop me after the service and ask, "Can't we sing some Christmas carols?" That happened so regularly that after a few years, I started opening the service on the second Sunday with an Advent hymn, but then I used carols for the second and final hymns. On the third Sunday, I again employed a mix of Advent and Christmas songs, but by the fourth Sunday, it was all Christmas carols.

The problem is that Advent is out of sync with our culture. On the church calendar, the liturgical year begins with Advent, which starts four Sundays before Christmas Day. On the street, however, the weeks leading up to December 25 are the "Christmas season," for which Christmas music, both secular and sacred, is the soundtrack. Thus, to be singing Advent music in church during that period seems to many to be discordant. And if I had insisted on linking our hymns slavishly to the liturgical calendar, I wouldn't have put carols in the service until Christmas Eve. I'd have then used them for all the music for the next two Sundays—covering the time period the church calendar designates as the "season of Christmas"—exactly when the rest of the world had moved on to other music, putting the church at variance with the culture once more.

I've often thought that the real problem with Advent hymns is not the competition from carols, but the fact that Advent doesn't have a primary theme the way Christmas does with its birth-of-Christ story. In fact, even the origins of Advent as a liturgical season are obscure.[1]

There are, however, some parallels between Advent and Lent, with each being a preparatory season for the one to follow—Advent for Christmas and Lent for Easter. Lent is better known as a time for penitence and renewal, whereas Advent tends to be overshadowed by the secular "Christmas holidays," but that's even more reason to take meditative Advent breaks from the roar of the festivities to focus on spiritual growth and renewal.

I said that Advent doesn't have a primary theme the way Christmas does. What I didn't yet say is that Advent has *several* good themes nonetheless. And they are so worthwhile that we shouldn't run unthinkingly through this season without considering what they might mean for our faith and our lives.

So as a way both to grasp the great themes of Advent in their own right and to experience Advent as spiritual preparation for Christmas, I've chosen to talk about the themes as *highways*, which are for traveling on and moving through somewhere to get from one place to another. A highway can be thought of as a *corridor,* which is also a synonym for a hallway, gallery, or some other indoor passageway. Sometimes it designates a place where a cluster of certain activities take place. For example, officials of the city of Akron, Ohio, not far from where I live, sometimes refer to it as a "biomedical corridor," noting that there are more than 600 biomedical businesses in the area.[2] *Corridor* is also used outdoors to describe a continuous strip of land that enables transit though a large area, such as the path of a highway. The root word from which *corridor* developed means "to run."[3] We run our cars, trucks, motorcycles, bicycles, and sometimes our feet on the highways of life, often without seeing what we run through in order to reach our destination. I'm not trying to rush you through Advent. I want your journey through this liturgical season to be filled with understanding, appreciation, gladness, and growth in God's Spirit. Come, travel the highways of Advent with me. And pay attention to the scenery!

Stan Purdum
Advent 2014

1 From "Advent," *The New Westminster Dictionary of Liturgy & Worship*, edited by Paul Bradshaw (Westminster John Knox Press, 2002); page 2.

2 From "Get the facts," Akron Biomedical Corridor, *www. akronbiomedicalcorridor.com/why-akron/get-the-facts.aspx*.

3 From "Corridor," in *Origins: A Short Etymological Dictionary of Modern English*, second edition, by Eric Partridge (Macmillan, 1959); page 122.

The Straightened and Leveled Highway

Scripture: Isaiah 40:1-11; Luke 3:1-14

US Route 62 starts in Niagara Falls, New York, and ends in El Paso, Texas. In between, it passes through ten states and runs variously on rural roads, city thoroughfares, small-town streets, two-lane blacktops, four-lane expressways, and occasionally, even on interstate Super-Slabs. Because of its angled course across the country, in some places, Route 62 is designated as an east-west road and other places as a north-south road. Yet there's one constant, one factor that makes it a *highway*: Along its entire 2,248 miles, it's always marked as US 62. That means, even without a map, you should be able to follow it from Niagara Falls to El Paso simply by paying attention to the signage.

The US Numbered Highway System has been in effect since 1926. It's a great convenience for travelers, especially when we're passing through places we've never been before, though we likely take the system for granted today. You may not know, however, that since 1955, AASHTO (American Association of State Highway and Transportation Officials), the body responsible for designating federal routes, has considered the system essentially complete. In other words, they're neither looking for new routes to number nor pushing for new roads to be built. In fact, several routes have been decommissioned (most notably, US 66, which has been largely replaced by a series of interstate highways). What's more, the remaining numbered routes are often being straightened—so much, in fact, that across the system, several hundred miles have been removed from those highways without changing the end points. I mentioned that US 62 is 2,248 miles long, but when it was first made a numbered highway, it ran for 2,289 miles. It still starts and ends in the same places, however. US 52 was originally 2,123 miles; it's now 2,072, but it still stretches from Charleston, South Carolina, to Portal, North Dakota.[1]

As this highway straightening has taken place, the ride on these routes has gotten a lot smoother as well. A few years ago, I pedaled my bicycle the full length of US 62, and I saw some of this leveling taking place. Here's how I described it in a book I wrote about the journey:

> A few miles northwest of Harrison, [Arkansas], . . . I found the road under construction, being widened from two lanes

to four. The old road, still in place, sustained the current traffic and apparently was to be retained as the westbound lanes. The new road would become the eastbound lanes, with a grassy strip between old and new. Clearly, the new portion was being built to newer standards than the original road, and I soon came to a spot where the difference was obvious. From the bottom of a hill, I could see the old road climbing its way upward in irregular fashion, humping over the contours of the land. The new lanes, however, climbed steadily because the irregularities had been scraped and filled. Also, the modern lanes didn't have to go as high because the very top of the hill had been lopped off.[2]

Having seen that road improvement underway, it occurred to me then that a few lines from Isaiah 40 could almost be the instructions in a highway engineer's manual:

Clear the LORD's way in the desert!
　Make a level highway in the wilderness for our God!
Every valley will be raised up,
　and every mountain and hill will be flattened.
Uneven ground will become level,
　and rough terrain a valley plain. (verses 3-4)

The prophet who spoke those words wasn't talking about actual highway construction, but about a preparation of mind and emotions to be in tune with a new thing God was about to do. That new thing was God's return to be with the people of Israel.

A Highway for God

But we're getting ahead of the story. In 586 B.C., the Babylonian army had conquered Jerusalem, destroyed the Temple and much of the city, and ended the Hebrew kingdom of Judah, of which Jerusalem was the royal capital. Leading citizens of Judah had been sent to exile in Babylon, where they remained for decades in captivity. This was a dark time for the Jews, many of whom understood the defeat and exile as punishment for their sins against God and evidence that God had left them to their fate and was no longer with them.

Sometime between 550 and 538 B.C., however, a prophet in exile with them began proclaiming a new message, the heart of which is contained in Isaiah 40:1-11. In that passage, the prophet pictures God commanding an unspecified *someone* to

Speak compassionately to Jerusalem,
  and proclaim to her that her compulsory service has
  ended,
that her penalty has been paid,
that she has received from the LORD's hand double for all
her sins! (verse 2)

That someone is also to be a "voice" crying out the highway-clearing message of verses 3-4 and announcing that "all humanity" will see God's glory, as verse 5 notes. While that someone remains unidentified, it's likely that it's a heavenly messenger (or messengers, since the Hebrew verbs are all plural imperatives). Thus, Isaiah 40:1-5 is a description of God in his heavenly council giving instructions to messengers waiting to do his bidding. The exiles would not have had difficulty believing that a prophet could witness the workings of God's council, for Jeremiah 23:18 indicates that true prophets were those who "stood in the LORD's council to listen to God's word . . . and announced it."

The heavenly message the prophet announces is: 1) God is returning to the people, restoring their relationship with God, and 2) their years of captivity will soon end and they will be permitted to return to Judah. In that context, the highway metaphor of verses 3-5 would seem to be especially apropos. Since going home would require a long and arduous journey across "desert" and "wilderness," both of which are referenced in verse 3, we might assume this message is saying that God is going to ease their journey through the geographic corridor between Babylon and Judah. In fact, in Isaiah 35:8-10 there is a spiritualized description of a "highway" over which the exiles can return to "Zion" (Jerusalem). But that's not the highway the "voice" is speaking of in Isaiah 40:3-4. There, it's the way over which the Lord will pass as he comes back to the people, and the heavenly hosts are to make it straight and level so that nothing impedes God from getting to his chosen ones.

The event to which Isaiah 40:1-11 alludes became a historical reality in 538 B.C., a year after the Persians defeated the Babylonians and swept their lands into the Persian Empire. Persia's King Cyrus issued an edict granting permission for any of the exiles who wished to do so to return to Judah, reclaim their homes, and rebuild Jerusalem and the Temple. Many of the Jewish captives took advantage of this.

If Isaiah 40 refers to a long-ago restoration, an event that was several centuries back even when Jesus was born, why is it one of the traditional readings for Advent? That's because when John the Baptist came on the scene to announce the arrival of the Messiah, faithful observers identified him as the "voice" in the wilderness calling for the preparation of a roadway for the Lord. Luke makes this connection in Chapter 3 of his Gospel, quoting Isaiah 40:3-5 (Luke 3:4-6). Matthew and Mark both identify John as the voice from Isaiah 40:3 as well (Matthew 3:3; Mark 1:1-8). In the Gospel of John, the Baptizer himself says he is that voice (John 1:23).

Leveling and Straightening

We'll talk more about John the Baptist in "The Highway of Enthusiasm," but for now, we note that in the New Testament, his is the voice calling for leveling and straightening the highway to speed the arrival (that is, the Advent) of God's Messiah. We should not miss, however, that John addresses a different "road crew" from the one the Isaiah voice does. The voice in the Isaiah reading directs *the heavenly hosts* to level and straighten God's highway; in the Gospels, John directs *the people in his audience* to do the roadwork—*in their own lives.* Luke says that John called for "people to be baptized *to show that they were changing their hearts and lives and wanted God to forgive their sins*" (Luke 3:3, italics added). And as we continue reading in Luke 3, we hear John tell his audience, "Produce fruit that shows you have changed your hearts and lives" (verse 8).

John eventually becomes more specific: "Whoever has two shirts must share with the one who has none, and whoever has food must do the same" (verse 11). To tax collectors, noted as a group for overcharging people on their taxes and pocketing the difference, John says, "Collect no more than you are authorized to collect" (verse 13). To soldiers, known for abusing their authority over the populace and for being disgruntled, John says, "Don't cheat or harass anyone, and be satisfied with your pay" (verse 14).

Based on this pattern of calling for "leveling and straightening" in areas specific to one's opportunities, resources, and roles, we can assume that if John were addressing us, he'd tailor his directives to the actual circumstances of our lives as well, so that the highway for Christ to come to us is unobstructed. This is not to suggest that we build our own highway to Christ—that is the work of God—but once the initial highway is in place, there is a lot of leveling and straightening for us to do. That highway is still a path by which Christ can come to us, but like on the original routes of the US Numbered Highway System, we often force him to travel some significantly bumpy, potholed, and circuitous ways, and deal with gridlock and long no passing zones along the way.

For example, the hindrances on our spiritual highway can be such things as tightfistedness; failure to love our neighbors as we love ourselves; behaviors that don't measure up to the standards set by the Ten Commandments and the Sermon on the Mount; blindness to the needs of those around us; silence when our Christian testimony would help others in their spiritual journey; unchecked anger; failure to follow through on promises; sins of omission; halfhearted commitments; belittling remarks to loved ones; and so on. With a little thought, most of us can come up with our own list of places where we need to do some leveling and straightening. These are all human failings, and some may be outright sinful, though we may not have noticed. British author Monica Furlong points out how some of our sins may eventually become apparent:

> Sin strikes me as . . . not the rather fiddling obsession with envy and anger and small untruths that we often make it out to be, but something much more terrible—a determined obstinate choice of unreality and self-deception which has become a whole life-style. For the most part we are as unaware of it as we are unaware of our own appearance seen from the back view, too unaware to confess it. It is only when we catch a sudden glimpse of our own unreality through the distortions it may produce in our children, our marriage partners, or others who are close, that awareness breaks through. [3]

Perhaps none of our sins and failings is so flagrant as to completely close down the highway between the Lord and ourselves, but our sins and failings are obstacles that keep us from living fully as Jesus' disciples.

All of this makes Advent, when we traditionally read the texts about John the Baptist calling people to prepare the way for the Lord, an important time in our spiritual lives. In the introduction to this study, I noted that Advent can be considered a preparatory season for Christmas. That makes this a good time to consider the ways in which we can "produce fruit that shows [we] have changed [our] hearts and lives," as John called for (verse 8).

Help From the Highway Engineer

One form that spiritual growth can take is considering what detours, roundabout ways, and narrow places interfere with our discipleship, and then offering those rough spots to God with a prayer, such as "Lord, I'm trying to follow your Son, but my self-centeredness (or whatever) creates a bottleneck in my life. Help me to surrender this hindering sin and open a wider thoroughfare to your presence." Or we can start further back, praying for God to reveal to us where we've placed obstacles and detours on the highways through which Christ travels to us.

We should not be surprised that such obstacles and detours exist and are of our own making. Even if we've been through a born-again entryway to the Christian life, we weren't born fully matured Christians. There's a story about Pope Gregory I (A.D. 540-604) commissioning 30 monks to preach the gospel in Britain, telling them to be patient with the new converts since some of the desired changes in their habits and lifestyle would come about only gradually. I've not be able to verify that story, but it rings true, especially in light of something Gregory wrote that we can verify: "He who endeavors to ascend to the highest place, rises by degrees or steps, and not by leaps."[4] The writer of the epistle to the Hebrews said something similar, though his words were essentially a scolding to some Christians he thought weren't paying enough attention to their spiritual growth. He wrote, "You have come to the place where you need milk instead of solid food. Everyone who lives on milk is not used to the word of righteousness, because they are babies. But solid food is for the mature " (Hebrews 5:12-14). So our prayer could be for growth in our spiritual digestive system so that we can handle the solid food of mature faith. The late United Methodist Bishop Lance Webb once said, "All God's people are called to be 'saints in therapy,' in the process of being made perfect in love, growing from babes in Christ to mature adulthood, measured by nothing less than Christ's stature!"[5]

In my own case, impatience is a bottleneck I've become aware of on that spiritual highway. I've never been one to wait easily, but it's not just that I don't like waiting. I fume at doctors who leave me sitting in their waiting rooms beyond the hour of my appointment. I fidget when someone I have arranged to meet doesn't arrive at the designated time. If at all possible, I avoid catalog and online ordering, preferring instead to drive to the next town if necessary so that I can get the desired items right now. When I board an elevator, I sometimes press the door-close button right away to hurry things along. I'm bothered by drivers ahead of me who choose to drive slower than the posted speed limit. When I am ready to check out of a store, I always search for the line with the fewest people ahead of me. Still, I become quickly irritated when the person in front of me slows things up by not having his or her cash or credit card ready, or worse yet, has some item that requires a price check.

This impatience is not simply a personal characteristic; it's a sinful detour. I can become downright rude to people I think aren't moving fast enough, such that after blurting out some insensitive remark to move someone along in a supermarket check-out line, I've been glad that I wasn't wearing my church T-shirt (I certainly don't want someone thinking that such rudeness is acceptable in a Christian lifestyle). What's more, it's not lost on me that both patience and kindness are fruits of the Spirit (Galatians 5:22). I finally recognized my pushing of others for the hindering sin—the "bottleneck"—that it is, and took it to God in prayer. With God's help, I'm exercising more patience. But I have to work at it, and viewing Advent as a time for removing roadblocks on the spiritual highway is a good reminder for me to continue to keep patience and kindness on my prayer list.

Of course, it's not realistic to think we can remove the gridlocked places all by ourselves, but we should not discount what God will help us do. In fact, asking God for help with matters of character and righteousness is exactly what Jesus was talking about when he said, in the Sermon on the Mount, "Ask, and you will receive. Search, and you will find. Knock, and the door will be opened to you. For everyone who asks, receives. Whoever seeks, finds. And to everyone who knocks, the door is opened" (Matthew 7:7-8).

One reason we may find this advice hard to accept is if we hear it as some kind of guarantee that God will say yes to anything we ask for—"Just follow these instructions faithfully, pray with intensity and persistence, and you will get the desired results." But if we need evidence that such an interpretation is mistaken, we have only to recall that even such a devout and fervent follower of Jesus as the apostle Paul did not received a "yes" to at least one prayer request. "I was given a thorn in my body because of the outstanding revelations I've received so that I wouldn't be conceited," Paul explained in a letter to the Christians at Corinth. "I pleaded with the Lord three times for it to leave me alone. He said to me, 'My grace is enough for you, because power is made perfect in weakness'" (2 Corinthians 12:7-9).

So if Jesus' words about asking are not a guarantee that praying will get us what we ask for, what do they mean? Like most verses in the Bible, the meaning becomes clearer if we read them in context. In the Sermon on the Mount thus far, Jesus had already instructed his hearers to live righteously, to forgo anger, to shun retaliation, to avoid lust, to love their enemies, to forgive those who injure them, and to cease worrying about the future.

If you had been in the audience that day, what might have been going through your mind? Maybe something like, "Well, Jesus, that's all very nice, but how am I going to do those things? I can't even forgive my neighbor for holding loud parties when I'm trying to sleep, so how am I going to love my enemy? Then there is anger and lust. I don't want those things, but they overtake me when I am not expecting them. You might as well ask me to give up eating or breathing!"

Jesus, it seems, anticipates those questions and makes his comment about asking, searching, and knocking. He tells his audience to ask God for the ability to live righteously, to love their neighbors, to forgive those who hurt them, and so on. Those are the qualities that praying affects. Jesus tells them that the answer to our prayers often comes in the form of spiritual graces in our lives, not in material treasures or in God changing the course of events in our lives.

Jesus urged his listeners to clear the obstacles on the highway he travels to us by asking God for help. That's a worthwhile project for Advent.

Questions for Reflection and Discussion

1. How does the image of the highway speak to you about your relationship with God and your daily life of faith?

2. What kinds of leveling and straightening do you need to do? What obstacles to your full discipleship need to be addressed prayerfully with God?

3. Have you had times when you were especially aware that Christ had come to you? If so, what did you take away from those experiences?

4. If you've not had that awareness, does that mean that Christ has not been present with you? Why or why not?

5. In what sense are you a "saint in therapy"?

6. How does Christ help in your relationship with God?

7. When you pray, what do you hope will happen?

8. What steps will you take to make Advent more than simply a get-ready-for-Christmas period?

Prayer

Examine me, God! Look at my heart!
Put me to the test! Know my anxious thoughts!
Look to see if there is any idolatrous way in me,
then lead me on the eternal path! (Psalm 139:23-24)

Focus for the Week

Once you have identified some spiritual "leveling and straightening" that you need to do, devote at least one prayer each day this week to discussing those "highway projects" with God, the ultimate highway engineer.

1 See "Sequential List with Termini and Lengths in Miles," U.S. Highways From U.S. 1 to U.S. 830. *www.us-highways.com/us1830. htm.*

2 From *Playing in Traffic: America From the River Niagara to the Rio Grande, by Bicycle,* Expanded Edition, by Stan Purdum (CSS Publishing, 2004); page 148.

3 From *Anglican Digest,* Lent 1995, quoted in *Context,* July 1, 1995.

4 From a letter Pope Gregory sent to the Abbot Mellitus, then going into Britain. Cited by Bede (673735): *Ecclesiastical History of the English Nation,* Book I, Chapter XXX, *www. fordham.edu/halsall/ basis/bede-book1.asp.*

5 From "How Do We Reverse Our Soul Drain?" by Lance Web, in *Circuit Rider,* February 1982; page 9.

General Sources consulted for biblical accuracy but not quoted:
    New Interpreter's Bible, Volume VI; pages 334-339.
    New Interpreter's Bible, Volume VIII; pages 212-213.
    "Isaiah 40:1-11," in *The Lectionary Commentary: The First Readings,* edited by Roger E. Van Harn (William B. Eerdmans, 2001); pages 327-330.

Second Week of Advent

The Highway of Reversal

Scripture: Isaiah 64:1-9; Luke 1:39-56

"I never expected life to hurt so much." The woman speaking was a member of a church I was pastoring, and we were talking privately after a Sunday morning service. The day before, she had visited her son in the county jail where he'd been sent after roughing up his girlfriend.

I knew and liked her son. A few years earlier, he'd been in a confirmation class I'd taught, and I'd received him into the church. He'd been active in the youth group and had attended the youth Sunday school class regularly. But somewhere along the way, he started heading in a different direction. He began using drugs, ignoring his parents' instructions, and running with a rebellious crowd. He still displayed flashes of the promising teenager he'd been, but they were often overshadowed by his darker side.

His parents were good people, and I knew they were attentive parents. Their other children were respectful and doing well, but this son, by then a young adult, was breaking their hearts.

In time, thanks in large part to his parents never giving up on him, this son eventually left the downward path he was on, and today, he is a contributing member of society. But I know about the agony and sorrow his parents went through in the meantime.

No doubt, many of us can identify with his mother's statement, "I never expected life to hurt so much." If it's not because of a loved one who's gone off the rails, then it's because of illness or tragedy in our family, or because of unfair circumstances we've had to face, or because of baggage we carry from a scarred childhood, or because of selfish behavior by people in power, or . . . well, you get the idea. Just think of how many words in our language describe some sort of trouble: *sickness, suffering, accident, sin, crime, abuse, misfortune, setback, problem, hurt, disappointment, greed, dilemma, snag, hardship, adversity, distress, evil, frustration*—just to name a few. We need so many words because trouble comes in so many forms, and many of those forms cause us pain.

If any of this connects for you, you're ready for one of the messages of Advent: the message about reversal. The Highway of Reversal is a route that leads to Christmas, and by traveling it, we can arrive at Christmas with a greater understanding and appreciation of what Advent proclaims.

The Lament

Isaiah 64:1-9 is one of the church's traditional readings for Advent. It opens with a cry that echoes the life-can-hurt statement:

> If only you would tear open the heavens and come down!
>   Mountains would quake before you
>   like fire igniting brushwood or making water boil.
> If you would make your name known to your enemies,
>   the nations would tremble in your presence. (verses 1-2)

In terms of literary style, Isaiah 64:1-9 is part of a larger unit, a lament that begins at 63:7 and ends at 64:12. A lament can be described as an argument with God in which the speaker hopes to convince God to reverse the direction in which things are heading. In this lament, the speaker bemoans the pain of life and envisions how God "coming down" would turn things around.

The whole passage is from the section of Isaiah that originated among the Jewish exiles who had finally been permitted to return home to Judah from captivity in Babylon. While that would seem to be a reason for happiness, the facts on the ground were not conducive to rejoicing. Squatters and newcomers now held some of the properties that had belonged to the exiles' families, houses were in ruins, Jerusalem had no city walls, and fields had gone without cultivation for so long that they had to be cleared all over again. Few jobs existed, the economy was in tatters, Judah was now a province of the Persian Empire, and the Jews were a subject people who were aware of their spiritual and moral shortcomings (in verses 5-7, the speaker acknowledges the unrighteousness of the people). In all of this, they had learned how much life could hurt. If only God would come down and reverse how things stood!

In time, things did improve somewhat for the returnees and their descendants. Nehemiah led the people in rebuilding Jerusalem, and Ezra led a spiritual revival. The prophets Haggai and Zechariah spurred the rebuilding of the Temple. And with the passage of time, other important aspects of their lives came together. Still, Judah remained under the Persian Empire, and over the years, they were passed from one foreign power to another. Eventually, there was a period of independence; but before the New Testament era opened, the land had come again under a foreign power—this time the Roman Empire. By the time Jesus was born, the Jews were still longing for the reversal that the Isaiah passage had envisioned.

Looking at the opening line of the Isaiah passage, it's easy to see why the church reads Isaiah 64 as we approach Christmas. At Christmas, God *did* come down— in the person of Jesus. In fact, that's what the Incarnation means. But since one focus of Advent is on the time *before* Jesus came, Isaiah 64 invites us to hear and identify with those longing for reversal. While we are not returnees from exile, we know enough about the pain of life to long for some reversal of our circumstances as well.

The Magnificat

Another passage that's often read during Advent is
the story of Mary's visit to Elizabeth (Luke 1:39-56). This
account is preceded by the visit of an angel of the Lord to
Mary, announcing to her that she was to bear God's Son.
Once Mary got past the shock of both seeing an angel and
learning that she was to bear a child who would be God's
own, she humbly said, "I am the Lord's servant. Let it be
with me just as you have said" (Luke 1:38). Mary's visit
to Elizabeth is the next episode in Mary's story. The angel
had told Mary that her relative Elizabeth, who was well
past childbearing age, was pregnant with a son. Her child,
as we know, would be John the Baptist.

Luke tells us that Mary hurried to the town where
Elizabeth lived, and when she entered the house and
greeted Elizabeth, the child in Elizabeth's womb "leaped"
(verse 41). At that moment, the Holy Spirit came upon
Elizabeth and she began to speak an oracle, proclaiming
to Mary, "God has blessed you above all women" (verse
42). Still under the inspiration of the Spirit, Elizabeth
added that her unborn child's leap had been a jump for
joy (verse 44). Then referring to Mary, Elizabeth declared,
"Happy is she who believed that the Lord would fulfill the
promises he made to her" (verse 45).

Mary indeed believed the Lord. At that point, the Spirit
inspired Mary as well, and a song of praise flowed forth
from her (the lyrics are in verses 46-55). Her song begins,
"With all my heart I glorify the Lord!" Some other Bible

versions, such as the NRSV, word it, "My soul magnifies the Lord." In the church, Mary's song is called the *Magnificat,* which is the first word in the Latin translation of this passage. This line provides one of the reasons that Roman Catholic Christians sometimes pray to God *through* Mary (not pray *to* Mary), as a Catholic priest friend tells me, for they see her as magnifying or focusing intensely on the Lord.

Mary also sings, "I rejoice in God my savior" (verse 47). This tells us two things. First, Mary, young as we believe her to be, already had experienced enough of the pain of life to know her need for a deliverer (which is what *savior* means). Second, when she sings of the Savior, she is thinking of God, whom Jesus would later refer to as the "Father" (see, for example, Matthew 5:16). While savior came to be applied to Jesus as well (see, for example, Luke 2:11), that never implied that only the Son and not the Father was the source of salvation. Everything that Jesus did—preaching, teaching, healing, eating with sinners, dying on the cross and then defeating death—was according to the Father's intention, and so the word *savior* can properly be applied to both the Father and the Son. At this point in Mary's life, however, she does not yet know the Son who is in her womb, but she accepts that God has set a saving plan in motion, and so she rejoices in "God my savior."

Mary has already declared herself ready to fill her role in God's plan (Luke 1:38), and so in her song, she identifies herself as God's "servant" (verse 48). She is

God's servant in that she puts herself completely at God's disposal. While Protestants don't usually think of Mary as a *unique* magnifier of God in quite the way that Catholics do, it's worth noting that *magnifier* could be a description of what *every* Christian should be: someone who brings God into close focus for others.

In any case, Mary's praise of God in the song is grounded in confidence both in God's present activity ("He has looked with favor on the low status of his servant" [verse 48]) and in God's ancient promise ("He shows mercy to everyone, from one generation to the next" [verse 50]). The key point in Mary's song, however, is her stating that *the coming salvation will be a great reversal*:

> [God] has pulled the powerful down from their thrones
>   and lifted up the lowly.
> He has filled the hungry with good things
>   and sent the rich away empty-handed.
> He has come to the aid of his servant Israel. (verses 52-54a)

Mary is singing about things yet to happen, but she uses present-tense verbs. She is aware that God is already moving, and that what God is doing will set in motion dramatic reversals: God, sings Mary, brings down the mighty and exalts the lowly. God fills the hungry and sends the rich away empty-handed. God comes to the aid of Israel. Perhaps Mary sings of these things as already accomplished because one reversal has indeed already taken place: God has chosen Mary, one noted for lowliness, to be called "highly favored" by all future generations.

The church understands the *Magnificat* as an expression of the kind of salvation Jesus brings. It's a salvation that some—the proud and powerful who use their position for their own advantage at the expense of others—will not welcome because it brings justice, calling the unjust and unrighteous into account. For the humble and lowly, however, and for those suffering injustice, that salvation is truly *good news*.

The Great Reversal

Let's be clear; we're not intending to bash the rich. We are well aware that many people who are comfortable financially, and even many who are among the "super-rich," do a lot of good and may, in fact, be living a life pleasing to God. But we're also aware that such is not always the case and that, even today, capitalism is often not conducive to compassion and community. If the recession of 2008 taught us anything, it's that some of the powerful, particularly the financially powerful, were *not* looking out for the rest of us. What's more, we are also aware that wherever we are on the ladders of power or finance, we don't always do all the good we could do either.

Thus, despite Mary's use of the present tense when referring to great reversals, it may occur to us that such reversals still have not happened. Mary sang about a day when God, the savior, "filled the hungry with good things and sent the rich away empty-handed" (Luke 1:53). Our thought may be, *well, when is that?* Such reversals may happen from time to time, but it seems like the ranks of those who rise on the backs of others are constantly replenished.

Nonetheless, during Advent, we should take a moment to understand this concept of great reversal, for what Mary is saying in this song is that the redemption of the oppressed and the humbling of the powerful is frequently a sign of God's activity in the world. That Jesus was born in a stable instead of in a palace or the first-century equivalent of a hospital on the Upper East Side is an indicator of God at work.

What's more, we have experienced the inner sense that the things the world uses as markers of greatness and power—wealth, influence, acclaim, fame—are not the things that matter in life. That is part of the great reversal as well.

As we learn the story of Jesus, we also come to understand that his whole life and ministry is an extension of this great reversal theme. Christ won our salvation by losing his life; he achieved power by emptying himself and "taking the form of a slave" (Philippians 2:7). And we receive his salvation, not through our strength and accomplishments, but through our recognition of our weakness. Or, as the apostle Paul put it to the Corinthians, "But God chose what the world considers foolish to shame the wise. God chose what the world considers weak to shame the strong. And God chose what the world considers low-class and low-life—what is considered to be nothing—to reduce what is considered to be something to nothing. So no human being can brag in God's presence" (1 Corinthians 1:27-29).

This reversal theme also runs through Jesus' teachings, and it's especially evident in his parables where the supposedly good people are unmasked as not so good while those from whom little is expected do the right thing. Consider the good Samaritan parable (Luke 10:29-37). There, the priest and Levite, who in that society were among the elite, turn their backs on the beaten man at the roadside, while the despised Samaritan comes to his aid. Or think of the prodigal son story (Luke 15:11-32), where the wayward son gets a party while his stay-at-home but self-righteous brother does not. In the story of the rich man and Lazarus (Luke 16:19-31), the rich man ends up "tormented in the place of the dead" (verse 23) while the beggar Lazarus is taken to "Abraham's side" (verse 22). In the parable of the wedding banquet (Luke 14:8-11), the first-seated and the last-seated have their seating swapped. In Jesus' story of the great dinner (Luke 14:16-24), street people fill the places of the invited guests, and the invited guests end up being the outsiders.

There's also the parable of the Pharisee and the tax collector praying in the temple (Luke 18:9-14), where the boastful prayer of the highly placed Pharisee walls him off from forgiveness while the tax collector's humble prayer brings him God's justification. Jesus even ends that parable with words about reversal: "All who lift themselves up will be brought low, and those who make themselves low will be lifted up" (verse 14).

Traveling the Highway of Reversal

In the church, it's always important to hear the biblical lessons about reversal, but in the current time perhaps even more so. In many places, including in the United States, the church is not prospering in the kinds of things that are often counted as marks of success. Many congregations are down in numbers, and Christians are often seen by the larger world as ineffective do-gooders.

But this is the time to look anew at Mary's son. The trappings of success were never his goal. Jesus did not accomplish his work by winning. He came as a servant. His task was to bear witness to the love of God, not to win battles. We call him Lord, but he didn't come to lord it over us. During his final week, he became a victim—betrayed, arrested, condemned, and crucified. He became a powerless Christ.

Thus we, his followers, should understand that the message of the great reversal that Mary sang about and Jesus lived means that we ought not to count too much on such things as success, popular acceptance, and achievement. Certainly as a church, our real contribution to the world cannot be measured by numbers and image; it's measured by how well we have loved God and our neighbor—things that have nothing to do with power.

But we are in *Advent* now—and the word means coming, which implies that Advent is a waiting period, a time of looking forward to the appearance of the One who ushers in the great reversal. Mary's song is an Advent song. In her day, people were looking for a messiah who would bring a reversal, but the idea of the reversal many had was that the rich and powerful would become poor and weak while the poor and weak would become rich and powerful. In other words, they would exchange places.

But what good would that do? The world would be little different; we'd simply have different people in the same old roles. One reason many people did not accept that Jesus was the Messiah was because he was not interested in *that* kind of reversal. Rather, his great reversal, built on love, showed that the "weakness" demonstrated in such things as servanthood and compassion was the real strength and that "poverty" shown by not holding too tightly onto possessions was the real wealth.

That's what magnifying the Lord really means. We invest ourselves in the ways of service, humility, loving our neighbor, and so on; and because we do, people are able to see God more clearly. That's because, as Mary's song tells us, the great reversal of the world's values is a sign of the activity of God.

An old story makes this point. I hesitated to use it because it's been floating around in various versions, so who knows what the original was and if it even really happened. It also seems like too perfect an illustration to have really happened. But the spirit of it is true, so let me tell you the version I first encountered:

On a cold winter morning in Birmingham, a Christian woman noticed a small boy selling newspapers on the street. He had on old tennis shoes that were so ragged that she knew they couldn't be keeping his feet warm, and he had no socks at all. In fact, he was standing on a hot-air grate in an attempt to keep his feet from freezing. When she asked him why he hadn't worn warmer shoes, he said he didn't have any.

So the woman invited the boy to go with her into a nearby department store where she brought him a pair of new shoes and some socks. They boy seemed quite pleased, but he hurried out to finish selling his papers.

When the woman came back outside, the boy came over and thanked her, and then he asked her, "Are you God's wife?"

She was quite surprised, but she answered, "No. I'm just one of God's children."

To which the boy replied, "Well, I knew you must be some kin to him."

It's hard to imagine a boy old enough to be on the street being that naïve, but you get the point. In living and acting in the Spirit of Christ, we "magnify" God so that even those with poorer spiritual eyesight can see him. (And notice that the reply "I'm just one of God's children" could be a modern equivalent of Mary's "I am the Lord's servant" statement [Luke 1:38].)

Advent is the time of year when the church reads the *Magnificat*. It reminds us that pain and trouble do not get the last word. The great reversal is coming. The hungry will be filled; the lowly will be lifted; the weak will be made strong; and those who suffer will be made whole. That hope began with God's promise. It took a giant step forward at Christmas. It is the work of the church today.

Its full development will be when God's kingdom comes. In the meantime, we live with hope, brought by Jesus at Bethlehem and expressed in his suffering on Calvary. God is with us, and nothing can separate us from his love, not even pain and suffering. At Christmas, God planted the seeds of the great reversal, and during Advent, as we read Mary's song, we can also take comfort in and hope from the confidence her song expresses in the activity of God in this world.

As we face the problems of life, especially those that seem to defy solution—even when all we have left to do is muddle through—we do not muddle through alone. We can view our pains and losses and terrors and closed doors against the backdrop of this great song of faith from the lips of Mary.

I think Mary would have great sympathy and compassion for the woman who said, "I never expected life to hurt so much." But Mary's song implies that hurt never has the final word; *God does.*

We could call that word one of salvation, or of deliverance, or of healing. But for now, in Advent, it's enough to think of it as a word of reversal.

"If only you would tear open the heavens and come down!" cried the speaker in Isaiah.

"[God] has pulled the powerful down from their thrones and lifted up the lowly," answers Mary. "He has filled the hungry with good things."

Questions for Reflection and Discussion

1. In what ways have you found life to hurt more than you expected?

2. What would you like to see reversed in your life? In what ways does the confidence expressed in Mary's song address your wish for things to be turned around?

3. What things in society need to be reversed? Which of these does your commitment to follow Jesus call you to work on? What steps can you take in that direction?

4. In what ways do you seek to magnify the Lord, to bring him into close focus for others?

5. What effect does the "success" of your church (or lack of success of your church) have on your feelings about your church? What does the great reversal suggest about the church's future?

6. While the "are you God's wife?" story is probably a made-up account, what gospel truth do you hear in it?

Prayer

During this Advent season, O God, meet our human hurts with your divine help. Even where we can do nothing other than to muddle through our troubles, let your grace reverse for us the meaning of the difficulties of our lives, so that we may face them without despair. In Jesus' name we pray. Amen.

Focus for the Week

In your prayer times this week, allow the idea of a great reversal to shape your petitions to God for yourself, your family and friends, and the society in which you live. Consider how traveling through the Highway of Reversal might enable you to arrive at Christmas with a greater personal connection to what God did in sending Jesus to our world.

General Sources consulted for biblical accuracy but not quoted:
"Isaiah 64:1-9," *The Lectionary Commentary: The First Readings*, edited by Roger E. Van Harn (William B. Eerdmans, 2001); page 396.
New Interpreter's Bible, Volume IX; pages 54-56.
John Dominic Crossan, "Parables of Reversal," *In Parables: The Challenge of the Historical Jesus* (Harper & Row, 1973); pages 53-79.

The Highway In Between

Scripture: Isaiah 7:10-17; Revelation 21:1-7

I like to finish what I start. That applies to projects I've launched, goals I've set, promises I've made, journeys I've embarked on, outcomes I've envisioned, debates I've engaged, and more. The reality is, though, that despite determined effort and the best of intentions, finishing is not always possible.

It's likely you've found that to be true as well. Perhaps you have a former friend with whom you've had a falling out. You want to repair the relationship, and you make the first move, offering an apology, but the other person prefers to hang on to the grudge. No matter what you do or say, the other person will not allow the friendship to be repaired. That's a restoration effort started that cannot be completed, and your only choice is to live with the incompletion.

In one congregation that I pastored, I buried a man who died in his seventies. He and his wife had been married nearly fifty years and had seemed to have a good marriage. But when I was talking with his wife the day he died, she expressed sorrow that the last words she'd spoken to him had been snappish—nothing nasty, simply the kind thing any of us might say to our spouse in a moment of irritation. But it was not the last thing she wanted him to hear, and she now felt bad that she'd not said something more loving. It was an incompletion.

I was listening to a radio talk show, and a woman called in. She told the host that as a child and youth, she'd been sexually abused by an adult male relative. Like many abused people, she'd been ashamed and had not told anyone. But as an adult, she had gone through some counseling and now felt that she needed to confront her abuser to complete her emotional healing. The problem was that the abuser had died a few months previously, so there was no way for her to face down the man about what he'd done to her. It was an incompletion.

Sometimes in relationships and especially in marriage, we encounter matters in which we are in strong disagreement. If neither of us can persuade the other, we may choose, for the good of the relationship, to "agree to disagree" and move on. Under the circumstances, that may be the best we can do, but it leaves both parties with a sense of incompletion.

There are many other incompletions in life. How often are education tracks or career paths put on hold because life crises or unexpected opportunities intervene? How many jobs are left unfinished because unforeseen circumstances arise? How many promises have we made, fully intending to keep them, only to find that changed situations make that impossible? Life's incompletions, unresolved relationships, and unfinished business have a way of haunting us, sapping our energy, leaving us with regrets, and leeching joy away from new endeavors.

What's more, there are incompletions in *us*. Time and again we've resolved to be more patient, less argumentative, slower to anger, quicker to praise, less critical of others, and more generous in our judgment of them. And time and again we have failed to make those changes, at least in any consistent way.

While it is not usually identified as such, Advent is a season especially for those of us living with life's ragged edges. In fact, Advent itself is the story of unfinished business. Traveling the Advent highway called "In Between" brings us to a place where we can view life's incompletions in a context of hope—and even anticipation.

The First Advent

The word *advent* means coming or arrival, and the season of Advent focuses attention on two periods where incompletion is a dominant theme. The first period was the time beginning with the Hebrew prophets who announced the "someday" restoration of Israel to take place with the arrival of a Messiah, an agent of God who, it was hoped, would restore a united Israel to the independence and glory it once had under King David.

Isaiah 7:10-17, a traditional Advent reading, provides a starting point for messianic expectation. The prophet Isaiah lived at a time when the people of Israel were divided into two kingdoms, sharing the land that had formerly been the united kingdom under King David and his son, King Solomon. The northern group, consisting of ten tribes, retained the name Israel. The southern group, consisting of two tribes, took the name Judah. Isaiah was a citizen of Judah.

But these were troubled times, as the first nine verses of Isaiah 7 recount. The Assyrian Empire was rising, conquering smaller nations and seeking access to the commerce of the Mediterranean area. This latter goal put the Assyrians on a conquest path against Aram (roughly equivalent to modern-day Syria) and Israel (called "Ephraim" in Isaiah 7:2, after Israel's dominant tribe). In response, the kings of those two nations formed a military alliance and called on Judah to join them. When Judah's King Ahaz refused, the Aram-Israel alliance marched against Judah, intending to dethrone Ahaz, who was a descendent of David, and replace him with their own man, who was not of David's line.

Ahaz and the Judahites were understandably frightened by the looming incursion. But at that point, God sent Isaiah to Ahaz with a message that Judah had nothing to fear from the present threat. This threat, said Isaiah, would soon dissolve if Ahaz trusted God.

That brings us to verses 10-17, where Isaiah told
Ahaz to ask God for a sign that what Isaiah had declared
about the Aram-Israel threat would come to pass. Ahaz
declined to do so, not wanting to "test the Lord" (verse
12). But Isaiah gave him a sign anyway. Likely pointing
to a pregnant young woman who was nearby, Isaiah said
that she would give birth to a son who would be named
Immanuel (verse 14), which as the CEB footnote tells
us, means "God is with us." This child, said Isaiah, would
grow up to see Judah's enemies defeated and a king from
David's line still on Judah's throne. Although Isaiah was
speaking about a child who was in the womb right then,
later readers came to understand the prophecy as referring
to a *future* Messiah. Thus, more than a century later,
Jeremiah prophesied of a still-to-come Messiah: "In those
days and at that time"—that is, at an unspecified time of
God's choosing—"[God] will raise up a righteous branch
from David's line, who will do what is just and right in the
land" (Jeremiah 33:15).

More than 700 years after Isaiah told Ahaz that a
newborn named Immanuel would be a sign for the king,
Jesus was born, and his followers eventually concluded
that *he* was the fulfillment of the messianic prophecies of
Isaiah and Jeremiah. That's why when the Gospel writer
Matthew told of an angel announcing to Joseph that Mary
would bear God's Child, Matthew added that "all of this
took place so that what the Lord had spoken through the
prophet [Isaiah] would be fulfilled:

> Look! A virgin will become pregnant and give birth to a son,
>   And they will call him, Emmanuel.
> (Matthew 1:22-23, citing Isaiah 7:14).

English renderings of Isaiah 7:14 typically spell this name starting with an "I," while English renderings of Matthew 1:23 usually start it with an "E." In the Isaiah passage, biblical translators are working from Hebrew, the original language of the Old Testament. In the Matthew passage, they are working from Greek, the original language of the New Testament. The different spellings are because Hebrew and Greek use different vowels in this name.

In the Isaiah text, the Hebrew word the prophet used to describe the soon-to-be mother means young woman or lass or damsel rather than virgin, though of course, a lass or damsel could well be a virgin. This young woman, however, was already pregnant, and thus was not. Nonetheless, when Matthew cited this verse, he was using the Greek version of the Hebrew Bible called the *Septuagint*, where the Hebrew word had been rendered into Greek as virgin. While the word *virgin* is important to the account of the angel's message to Joseph regarding Mary's never-been-with-a-man state despite being pregnant, the larger point behind Matthew's recitation of Isaiah 7:14 is that Mary's soon-to-be-born child would be the embodiment of "God is with us"; he would be the long-awaited Messiah.

But one thing that means, of course, is that all those people who lived between Isaiah's time and the arrival (advent) of Jesus were living with *a giant incompletion.* They were living with the hope of a "someday Messiah," but that hope was not fulfilled in their lifetime.

The Second Advent

There is a sense in which Jesus' time on earth was a period moving toward completion. His last words, spoken from the cross, were "It is *finished*" (John 19:30, italics added). Finished is how many Bible versions render the underlying Greek word *teleō* (see, for example, the NRSV, NIV, and KJV). Today, however, *finished* is sometimes taken to mean, done for, wiped out, or dead. But though *teleō* was Jesus' final word as he breathed his last, he wasn't saying, "I'm done for." He was saying, "I have completed the work the Father has given me to do." And thus the Common English Bible, the most recent of the translations, gives Jesus' last words as, "It is *completed*" (italics added). For today's readers, completed accurately conveys the meaning of *teleō*, which is conclude, discharge (as a debt), or accomplish.

Nonetheless, while Jesus completed his work of salvation through his death and resurrection, in his post-resurrection appearances he made clear that there was much that wasn't completed. In the last post-resurrection instance Matthew records, Jesus told his followers, "Therefore, go and make disciples of all nations, baptizing them in the name of the Father and of the Son and of the Holy Spirit, teaching them to obey everything that I've commanded you. Look, I myself will be with you every day until the end of this present age" (Matthew 28:19-20). Obviously, one thing that was not completed, and still is not, is disciple-making; but beyond that, Jesus referred to "the end of this present age," which had not arrived then and has not arrived yet today either.

For Christians, the end of the present age is not doom, but the arrival of "a new heaven and a new earth" about which John of Patmos spoke in Revelation (21:1), where "there will be no mourning, crying, or pain" (Revelation 21:4). In other words, the kingdom of God will come in all its fullness. And for that kingdom to come, Christ must return. According to the Book of Acts, immediately after Jesus ascended, two angels told his followers, "Galileans, why are you standing here, looking toward heaven? This Jesus, who was taken up from you into heaven, will come in the same way that you saw him go into heaven" (Acts 1:11). Thus, the second period Advent focuses on began with the Ascension of the resurrected Jesus into heaven and continues until he comes again, his second arrival (advent).

A Season for Our Incompletions

As Jesus' return has not yet happened, we therefore live between the two advents of Jesus—the Incarnation and the Second Coming—a time when God's kingdom has not yet come in its fullness. It is a time of incompletion. That's why, in the Lord's Prayer, we pray "thy kingdom come," and why Charles Wesley's hymn, "Love Divine, All Loves Excelling," includes the plea, "Finish, then, thy new creation."[1] That's also why Advent is a season in tune with the incompletions of our lives and why I've called it the Highway In Between.

The "Jesus has already come" and "Jesus has not yet come again" focuses of Advent contribute to a certain lack of clarity in the observance of the season. Advent hymns, such as "O Come, O Come, Emmanuel" and "Come, Thou Long-Expected Jesus," are appropriate, but are they talking about the sketchily described hope of Israel in the long-ago past or our hope for a difficult-to-imagine return of Jesus in the nobody-knows-when future? Or both?

What's more, Christians are all over the board on how the Second Advent will play out. Some of us take it quite literally. Others of us see it as a way of conceptualizing the life-changing hope we find when accepting Christ individually. Yet others of us muddle in the middle, acknowledging that the Second Coming is too mysterious to comprehend fully, but it is still a place to anchor our hope when we're mired in the unfinished business of life.

No matter how we understand the Second Coming, here's what Advent proclaims: Whatever agonies and hard times the world may go through, however much the things we cannot bring to fruition frustrate us personally, in the kingdom to come, God completes his plan and it includes all those who are faithful to God. And in that kingdom, there are no more incompletions. Thus, as John of Patmos records it, in that kingdom, "the one seated on the throne said, 'Look! I'm making all things new. . . . *All is done'*" (Revelation 21:5-6, italics added).

In the Meantime

So what does it mean to be in transit on the Highway In Between? For one thing, it means we shouldn't hesitate to undertake good things simply because we may not be able to finish them. Certain practices in the business world illustrate this quite plainly. Back in 1982, Tom Peters and Robert H. Waterman, Jr. published a book called *In Search of Excellence* in which they reported what they'd discovered while studying the most successful companies (as judged by long-term profitability and continuing innovation). The book has never fallen out of use since then, and it continues to be popular today. According to Peters and Waterman, what differentiates the consistently successful businesses from less successful ones is a willingness to experiment and try things out before projects are in completed forms. In other words, they take an idea that is not fully developed and roll it out. The motto of these successful companies could almost be, "Do it, fix it, try it"[2] (or, as one executive at Cadbury's put it, "Ready. Fire. Aim."[3]).

Some of the less profitable businesses, in contrast, spend months or years planning new projects or products, but delay introducing them until they have eliminated every possible bug. If you are talking about developing a space shuttle, then anticipating every conceivable problem is vitally important, but in other things, getting most of the job done is often enough to find out if it will fly.

I tested this ready-fire-aim principle in a church. We'd conceived of developing a Sunday evening program for fourth, fifth, and sixth graders to run concurrently with our youth group meetings. For two years, we had talked about doing it, but we had delayed starting it while looking for leadership and debating whether Sunday evening was a good time for the program. Finally, using the ready-fire-aim philosophy, we just announced a starting date and began. What we quickly discovered was that there was not enough interest from the kids in a Sunday evening program to sustain it, and after a few weeks, we discontinued it. That left us free to turn our attention and energy elsewhere. If we had tried to get all the pieces in place before starting the program, we could have gone on putting a lot more work into something that wasn't going to fly no matter what we did. In this case, going live with our unfinished business led to a kind of resolution: letting the program go. (What we did not let go of, however, was our concern for the spiritual development of children, and we put some more effort into our Sunday school, where we already had the kids present.)

Could the same ready-fire-aim principle work in relationships? Might a halting, stammered, imperfect attempt to patch things up with a friend put the friendship back on track? You won't know until you try, but not trying is sure to leave the relationship festering.

The Highway In Between is a place where we discover that not everything started needs to be brought to completion, or at least not to completion right now. Advent reminds us that even God allows his kingdom to exist in an unfinished stage. At the beginning of his ministry, Jesus announced that the kingdom of God had begun. He said, "Now is the time! Here comes God's kingdom!" (Mark 1:15). On another occasion, when some Pharisees asked Jesus when the kingdom of God was coming, he answered, "God's kingdom isn't coming with signs that are easily noticed. Nor will people say, 'Look, here it is!' or 'There it is!' Don't you see? God's kingdom is already among you" (Luke 17:20-21). Yet he also talked about the kingdom coming in the future, after he returned, and the Book of Revelation describes the "new heaven and new earth"—all still to come—as that kingdom. The best thinking among Bible scholars is that both ideas about the kingdom are true: It is *both* yet to come *and* already here. The kingdom has begun and is present in the hearts of Jesus' followers, but it isn't here in its fullness yet.

The gospel message itself reminds us that past wrongs that can't be undone can be forgiven, and we can move on in newness of life with Christ. Nonetheless, the importance of *trying* to finish what we start has a value of its own. In fact, there is often *holiness* in the trying, even when we don't succeed. In his letters, the apostle Paul often gave advice about holy living, and thus to the Romans he wrote,

"If possible, to the best of your ability, live at peace with all people" (Romans 12:18). That's very practical instruction; Paul recognized that some attempts to live at peace can't be completed. But to the best of our ability, we should find out what's possible in that interaction.

There's a pertinent story about Igor Stravinsky. He was considered by many to be the greatest and most versatile composer of the twentieth century, but he also had a reputation for writing extremely difficult passages into his music. One time, he created a violin interlude so formidable that a master violinist assigned to perform it complained to Stravinsky that it was impossible to play.

"Of course," Stravinsky is said to have replied. "I don't want the sound of someone playing the passage. I want the sound of someone trying to play it."[4]

This Stravinsky story is usually considered apocryphal, but on the Snopes website, which attempts to determine the truth of things existing as urban legends, one respondent, using the web identity "Mouse," commented, "As a musician, I wouldn't be the least bit surprised if that turned out to be an actual quote. Stravinsky's a nightmare to play."[5]

While some of the unfinished business in our life is frustrating or disappointing, other incompletions may actually be nightmarish. We may be able to resolve some of them, but we will always have some stuff hanging, and often hanging uncomfortably.

It may be that we should think of the incompletions of life as gifts from God that are given so that we keep on striving and don't spend life standing on the sidelines. Indeed, what would our lives be without some unreached goals to strive toward?

But the most important thing we can do is take the unfinished things in our life to God and ask God for guidance to help us know the right choice: abandon them, keep trying, hand them off, bide our time, or live with them. In fact, there is a prayer used in Alcoholics Anonymous but written for the larger circumstances of life that asks just that:

> God grant me the courage to change the things I can,
> The serenity to accept the things I cannot change,
> And the wisdom to know the difference.

That could be a prayer for Advent, as we travel the Highway In Between, but it shouldn't be the *final* prayer of the season. That's because, ultimately, Advent is not about living with our incompletions, but about *resolution*. It points us to the day when God's kingdom comes and God says, "Look! I am making all things new" (Revelation 21:5). We may live with unresolved business in the meantime, but by God's grace, incompletions are not the end of our story. Instead, "all things new" are the opening words of our eternal story, and that helps us deal with the unfinished business in the interim.

There responsible for the effort, but we cant control the outcome.

Questions for Reflection and Discussion

1. Which of your projects or goals seem to be at a standstill? How might Advent be *your* season to find resolution?

2. What incompletions do you recognize in yourself? In what ways do you attempt to address them? What has worked? What has not?

3. How do the incompletions in your own makeup help when noticing the incompletions in others? Where do your incompletions interfere with your relationships?

4. What do you understand the Second Coming to mean? What role does it play in your Christian faith and practice?

5. What projects are you pursuing where a ready-fire-aim approach might move them toward completion?

6. In what ways might your incompletions be a gift from God? What might they be teaching you?

Prayer

Be present, O Lord, in my struggles to get things done. Help me especially when I face matters that resist completion. When it is your will that I see a matter

"Trees" by Joyce Kelmer

through, give me courage and creativity. Help me to know when laying aside a matter is the right thing to do. And for those irresolvable things that I must not put down, give me your grace to live with them. Your kingdom come. In Jesus' name we pray. Amen.

Focus for the Week

This week, as you come up against an incompletion, prayerfully consider what ought to be the next step: Should you abandon it, keep trying, hand it off, bide your time, or live with it?

---

1 From *The United Methodist Hymnal* (Copyright © 1989 by The United Methodist Publishing House); 384.

2 From *In Search of Excellence*, by Tom Peters and Robert H. Waterman, Jr. (Harper & Row, 1982); page 134.

3 From *In Search of Excellence*; page 119.

4 Told by Sue Shellenbarger, "'I'll Never Put You in a Nursing Home': The Promises One Should Never Make," *The Wall Street Journal*, July 1, 2004, D1.

5 From *http://msgboard.snopes.com/message/ultimatebb.php?/ubb/get_topic/f/101/t/000313.html*. Accessed July 29, 2013.

General Sources consulted for biblical accuracy but not quoted:

Harper's Introduction to the Bible, by Gerald Hughes and Stephen Travis (Harper & Row, 1981); pages 55-56.

"Isaiah 7:10-16," in *The Lectionary Commentary: The First Readings*, edited by Roger E. Van Harn (William B. Eerdmans, 2001); pages 310-313.

The New Interpreter's Bible, Vol. VI (Abingdon, 2001); pages 106-113.

"Messiah," in *The Dictionary of Bible and Religion*, edited by William H. Gentz (Abingdon, 1986); pages 683-684.

"*Teleō*" (G5055), in *Strong's Talking Hebrew & Greek Dictionary* (in WORDsearch 7 computerized Bible program).

Michael H. Burer, "Immanuel vs. Emmanuel, or A Question of Translation Philosophy," Bible.org. *http://blogs.bible.org/netbible/ michael_h._burer/immanuel_vs._emmanuel_or_a_question_of_ translation_philosophy*. Accessed July 30, 2013.

Fourth Week of Advent

The Highway
of Enthusiasm

Scripture: Matthew 3:1-12; John 1:6-8, 19-28

Given the title of this chapter, I feel the need to issue a disclaimer: I am not attempting to be a cheerleader for Jesus.

Don't get me wrong. I don't mean that I'm not strongly convinced about the gospel of Jesus Christ or that I'm unwilling to share my faith. But I do mean I'm not trying to function as a cheerleader, stoking up hurrahs from a crowd that may or not be excited about a team on the field. I'm not waving a pompom and shouting, "LET'S HEAR IT FOR JESUS! GIMME A 'J.' GIMME AN 'E.' . . . "

So, despite the fact that "enthusiasm" is usually used to describe an emotion, the message of this chapter is not that we should all get more excited about our faith in Jesus Christ (though if that happens, great!). The fact is, many Christians get a bit uneasy when someone starts talking about emotions and faith together. That's in part because of a longstanding divide within the church at large about whether faith is more a matter of the emotions or of reason. People who lean one way tend to make people who lean the other way uncomfortable.

I have long been in the reason camp. One of the factors that attracts me to writing as well as preaching is that I value the power of explanation, which, of course, requires reasoning. (I sometimes describe myself both as a *proclaimer* of the faith and as an *explainer* of it.) But the church I grew up in, while not ignoring the head side of faith, placed great value on the heart side. Virtually every service in that denomination included an altar call. In the way these were conducted, with the singing of invitational hymns and the coaxing words of the preacher, they sometimes seemed to me to be overly dependent on snagging the emotions of the worshippers. And I recall one preacher who, every time he talked about what Jesus did for the world, would start to cry right there in the pulpit. As a young person witnessing this, I found it embarrassing.

On various levels, that thinking-feeling dichotomy continues in the church today. One of the differences between what we call a *traditional service* of worship and what we call a *contemporary service* is that the former often seems to have more elements to connect with the mind and the latter often seems to have more elements to connect with the emotions. Of course, both intend to connect with head *and* heart, but the difference is one of emphasis; and that's probably a good thing, since not all of us respond to God through the same avenues. Still, some people wonder how you can have an adequate worship service without a reasonable presentation of the faith. Others wonder how you can have an adequate worship service without feeling something tugging on your heartstrings or at least moving your feet to tap a little.

What's more, there is biblical precedent for both. Some of us like Isaiah 1:18, "Come now, let us reason together . . ." (RSV), while others prefer Psalm 150:3-4, "Praise God with lute and lyre! / Praise God with drum and dance!"

I would suggest that the Advent Highway of Enthusiasm is a place that brings reason and emotion together and conveys us to Christmas with head and heart in tune.

John the Baptist, Fiery Preacher

Jesus, of course, is the central figure of Christmas. In Advent, though, it's his forerunner, John the Baptist, who takes center stage, though it's clear he has no desire to upstage Jesus. Rather, he labors to prepare the way for Jesus. John is the main character in both of the Scripture passages listed for this chapter, and both are traditional readings for Advent.

Although John is the subject in each case, the two passages give us different pictures of the man. In Matthew 3, he's a firebrand, dressed in rough clothing and living on a sparse diet of locusts and wild honey, who confronts people throughout Judea. He calls them to confess their sins and repent, and he baptizes them after they do. But when some members of the two religious sects, Pharisees and Sadducees, arrive on the scene, he calls them "children of snakes." The CEB says these two groups "came to be baptized by John" (Matthew 3:7), but it's unclear why any Pharisees and Sadducees, who elsewhere in the Gospels give no evidence of being convinced by John, would seek his baptism. The actual Greek of this verse is ambiguous; it only says that John saw them "coming to his baptism." Thus, the NIV says that they were "coming to where he was baptizing," which could mean that they merely showed up to see what was going on.

Whatever the reason for their appearance at this point, John confronts them by asking rhetorically who had warned them to "escape from the angry judgment that is coming soon?" (verse 7). If they have actually come to be baptized, they apparently want to skip the confession-of-sin and repentance steps, for John plainly tells them they have to start doing things that show they "have changed [their] hearts and lives" (verse 8). If they have come only to inspect what John is doing, his message still applies. Either way, he punches at their self-righteousness and anticipates that they might appeal to their "chosen" status as descendants of Abraham (that is, to their being Jews, God's chosen people) to excuse them from confession and repentance. Thus, John blasts them with "and don't even think about saying to yourselves, Abraham is our father. I tell you that God is able to raise up Abraham's children from these stones" (verse 9).

Then, comparing good works and righteous deeds to the "good fruit" of a tree, he tells them "every tree that *doesn't* produce good fruit will be chopped down and tossed into the fire" (verse 10, italics added). The Pharisees and Sadducees surely understand he's talking about *them*.

Even as John turns to his announcement of the "one who is coming after me," he continues pounding the Pharisees and Sadducees. He does not refer to the Coming One as compassionate, but as "stronger than I am" (verse 11). John's implication seems to be, "If you think I'm being tough on you, just wait until the one coming next arrives!"

Matthew never tells us directly what John's emotional state is during all of this, but from John's powerful words and energetic sentences, it is clear that this is not a dispassionate lecture; except for the fact that John's comments are right on target, they could almost be a diatribe.

John the Baptist, Rational Interviewee

In contrast to the picture of the Baptizer we get from Matthew 3, John 1 portrays a calm, reasonable man having a patient conversation with some priests and Levites. The priests were likely Sadducees, since that was the sect to which Jewish priests belonged, but here, John doesn't slam them as he did in the Matthew text. This passage also makes no mention of John's rough clothing and spartan diet.

This delegation of religious professionals had been "sent" to Jesus, by "the Jewish leaders in Jerusalem" (John 1:19) to learn more about John. The "Jewish leaders in Jerusalem" included the Pharisees (verse 24), but the phrase may have meant the Sanhedrin, the highest judicial and ecclesiastical council of the Jewish people at that time. Its membership included both Sadducees and Pharisees, under the controlling influence of the high priest. This council made it its business to vet anyone claiming to be a prophet or the Messiah. While John was making no such claim, the very size of the crowds he was drawing with his preaching probably impelled the Jewish leaders to check him out.

Thus, when these priests and Levites come to John and ask him, "Who are you?" they're not inquiring about his family identity. In fact, they almost certainly already know that. John's father, Zechariah, had been, like some of them, a priest (Luke 1:5), and even if he was deceased by the time John was an adult (which is likely; he was "very old" when John was conceived [Luke 1:7]), he would still be remembered by some of his younger colleagues.

So when this deputation asks John who he is, he quickly surmises that they want to know if he *thinks* he is the Messiah. He immediately and straightforwardly dispels that notion: "I'm not the Christ," he says. (John 1:20; the NRSV translates his response as "I am not the Messiah." Both "Christ" and "Messiah" carry the same meaning here—"anointed"—and are interchangeable terms.)

"Then who are you?" they ask. "Are you Elijah?" Elijah's time on earth had been more than 800 years before John's, but he had been transported directly to heaven in a windstorm without dying (2 Kings 2:11). This fueled an expectation among some Jews that he would return to signal the arrival of the messianic age.

John is not Elijah, but it's understandable that his questioners might wonder if he was. Jesus later said that John was Elijah (Matthew 11:14; 17:10-13), though he was probably speaking metaphorically. In the announcement to Zechariah that he would have a son, the angel said that son would be "equipped with the spirit and power of Elijah" (Luke 1:17), but he did not say that John would actually *be* Elijah. In any case, John remains unruffled as he tells his questioners that he's not that ancient figure come again.

"Are you the prophet?" they ask. This individual is unnamed because he's identified in the Hebrew Scriptures only by function. In Deuteronomy 18, Moses tells the Israelites that after they have entered the Promised Land, "The LORD your God will raise up a prophet like me from your community, from your fellow Israelites. He's the one you must listen to" (Deuteronomy 18:15). In John's day, some Jews believed this prophet to come would be the Messiah.

John plainly replies that he is not that prophet.

Well, then, "Who are you?" the delegation demands, adding, "We need to give an answer to those who sent us" (John 1:22).

John replies by describing himself as a *voice*, citing Isaiah 40:3: *"I am a voice crying out in the wilderness, / Make the Lord's path straight . . . "* (verse 23). This "voice" identity is a point in common with the Matthew 3 reading (verse 3). There, it's the narrator, Matthew, rather than the Baptizer himself who quotes Isaiah 40:3 and applies it to John, but the agreement between the John and Matthew passages about the Baptizer's role is clear.

The delegation isn't finished with John yet, however. They want to know, if he isn't the Christ, Elijah, or the prophet, why he is *baptizing* people. Jewish rites included baptism, but not for people who were born Jews; baptism was used for Gentiles who were entering into Judaism. Albert Barnes, an astute biblical commentator from the nineteenth century, wrote that the Pharisees "believed that those [Jewish] rites might be increased, but they did not suppose that it could be done except by the authority of a prophet or of the Messiah."[1] But here's John, who denies being a prophet or the Messiah, asking *everybody*, Gentiles and Jews alike, to be baptized.

John responds that he baptizes with water, but that one far greater stands among them, whom they have not yet recognized for who he is (verse 26). He means Jesus, of course, and the implication is that the arrival of Jesus is so momentous that everybody needs to be cleansed to be ready for it.

Throughout this entire encounter, John's answers are direct and even terse, but they are always reasonable.

Was John Enthusiastic?

Like most of us, John was neither all firebrand nor all rationalist, but both aspects of his personality served to

help him be a witness, a voice, testifying to the light that
is Jesus. In fact, John the Gospel writer stated that role
specifically: "A man named John was sent from God. He
came as a witness to testify concerning the light, so that
through him everyone would believe in the light" (John
1:6-7). Significantly, the Gospel writer adds one more
"not" about John: "He himself wasn't the light" (verse 8).

Now, a question: Do you think John was enthusiastic
about his work?

Perhaps you've never considered that question before,
but anybody who would live the ascetic life, wear coarse
camelhair clothing, and eat locusts and wild honey, as
John did, has to be considered a zealot, doesn't he? And
what is zeal but enthusiasm in overdrive?

But before you answer the question about John,
consider the history of the word *enthusiasm*. According
to the *American Heritage Dictionary*, "Enthusiasm
first appeared in English in 1603 with the meaning
'possession by a god.' The source of the word is the
Greek *enthousiasmos*, which ultimately comes from the
adjective *entheos*, 'having the god within.'"[2] Defined that
way, it would seem certain that John was enthusiastic
about his ministry. He was clearly inspired by God in his
pronouncements about Jesus and passionate in his call for
repentance.

But in the years since *enthusiasm* entered English, its
meaning has broadened. It moved first from "possession
by a god" to mean "a rapturous inspiration like that
caused by a god." Then it came to mean "an overly

confident or delusory belief that one is inspired by God," and then to mean "ill-regulated religious fervor, religious extremism." Only in more recent times did the word move to the familiar sense of "craze, excitement, a strong liking for something."[3]

In England during the 1700's, *enthusiastic* still implied ill-regulated religious fervor, religious extremism. When John Wesley, the founder of Methodism, was carrying out his ministry, one of the upper-class women who encouraged his work was Lady Selina Shirley, the Countess of Huntingdon. She was a woman of strong Christian faith, and when she died in 1791, the following inscription was placed on her tomb: "She was a Godly, righteous, and sober Lady, bounteous in good works and Christian affections, a firm believer in the Gospel of our Lord and Saviour Jesus Christ, and devoid of the taint of enthusiasm."[4] And that latter phrase was a compliment!

Today, you can have an enthusiasm for almost anything from bird watching to basket weaving, from cycling to crocheting, from sculpting to skydiving, from archery to zoology—and much more—without religion or God entering into it in any sense. By *that* definition, John may not have been enthusiastic at all. It depends on how you define the word. But if *enthusiasm* means "possession by a god," as the word once intended; and if we specify that the god involved is the one and only God of heaven and earth, then John was surely enthusiastic. He faithfully announced the coming of the Messiah, confronted those who because of self-righteousness weren't getting the message, and declared himself unworthy to carry the sandals of this Coming One. That sounds to me like being possessed by God.

Enthusiastic People

Now let's turn the question on ourselves. Defining enthusiasm as "allowing God to possess us," are you enthusiastic about your faith? I believe Christ needs enthusiastic people, but if you're not a demonstrative person, don't be too quick to say you're not enthusiastic.

If you are someone who readily feels the excitement of faith, if your relationship with Jesus makes you want to shut your eyes and raise your hands to heaven as you sing, or shout "Amen!" or dance in the aisles for that matter, that's fine. I, for one, welcome your emotional expression of how deeply you feel about the reality of Jesus in your life. (What's more, as an adult, I'm a lot more understanding of someone who is moved to tears by his or her faith than when I was a teenager seeing the weeping preacher.)

But if, like me, you are not particularly emotional, don't think this statement about Christ needing enthusiastic people leaves you out, for enthusiasm and passion are displayed through more channels than just the emotions.

To illustrate that, here are a few lines from an obituary that appeared in *The New York Times* in December of

2005. The deceased was Howard Gotlieb, who had been an archivist for Boston University:

> Howard B. Gotlieb, a Boston University archivist who cajoled, charmed, wheedled and—most effectively, he said—groveled to snare the papers of notables like the Rev. Dr. Martin Luther King Jr. and Bette Davis, not to mention Fred Astaire's dancing shoes, died Thursday at a Boston hospital. He was 79.[5]

Farther on in the obituary, it says Gotlieb had an "exuberant public personality," so maybe he was emotional about his work. But even without knowing that, we can tell he was enthusiastic about it. You don't cajole, charm, wheedle, and grovel for things you don't care deeply about.

I know a woman I'll call Sandy who goes to church regularly, where she can be seen lifting her hands heavenward during prayers and songs. She is easily moved by touching stories, appeals for charity, the personal troubles of fellow worshippers, and the like. She has participated in mission trips the congregation sponsored, and she returned from one in tears due to the depth of the experience she'd had helping others. She's also a member of a church team involved in prison ministry. There she has to be especially careful because she's a sucker for sad stories, and the prisoners have no shortage of those. Sandy has no problem saying she loves the Lord, and her life matches her testimony. I'd call her enthusiastic about her faith.

But I also think of a member of the last church I pastored, a man named Phil, whom I came not only to respect but also to consider a friend. No one who knew him would describe Phil as a starry-eyed romantic. I cannot imagine Phil waving his arms in a worship service. He was one of the most matter-of-fact people I have known—so unemotional, in fact, that people who didn't know him well sometimes assumed he was uninterested in what they were saying, when that wasn't the case. When we wanted somebody to read the Scriptures in the service, Phil was among those who said, "I'll do it." When our adult class needed a teacher, Phil stepped forward. After he accepted that responsibility, he took the time each week to print out the Scripture, read the lesson, look up additional information, and even bring in a joke he'd found to begin the class. Later, when we decided that our church should have a website, Phil gave his time to learn how to build one and make it happen. Phil had fought cancer for quite a while, but eventually nothing more could be done. Yet he showed up in worship week after week, even when he knew his days were numbered. People don't put out that kind of effort and energy for things they don't care deeply about. I'd describe Phil as enthusiastic about his faith.

Phil had a different temperament than Sandy, but for both, their enthusiasm for Christ was/is a warm place between hot, unfocused fanaticism and cold, unfeeling rationality.

Yes, Jesus needs enthusiastic people. The enthusiasm of John the Baptist is a mood and an attitude of

Advent. From him, we can learn that *enthusiasm* is not merely a feeling; *it is allowing God to possess us.* For some, that enthusiasm will demonstrate itself in some emotional expression, but we also see it in persistence, in perseverance, in stepping up to the plate, in showing up, in the things we gladly spend our energy on, and in the depth of our commitments.

Traveling the Advent Highway of Enthusiasm can bring us to Christmas with delight, ready to celebrate what God did in sending Jesus as the light to our world. It can also help us be ready to be a witness to that light.

Questions for Reflection and Discussion

1. Which of the two Gospel portrayals of John connect best for you? Why?

2. What would John likely say to you if you presented yourself to him for baptism?

3. In terms of temperament, are you more like Sandy or Phil? What does it mean for you to follow Jesus with both head and heart? How do the two work together to help you live as Jesus' disciple?

4. In what ways does the statement "enthusiasm is the warm place between hot, unfocused fanaticism and cold, unfeeling rationality" help you see enthusiasm as a quality worth seeking?

5. What does your enthusiasm for Jesus Christ call you to do in the coming year?

6. In what ways can your Christian witness be more on target by, like John, stating what you are *not*? (For example, I began this chapter by saying, "I am not attempting to be cheerleader for Jesus." My intention was to disarm readers who, from the chapter title, may have expected the lesson to be a call for each of us to dredge up more zeal and been turned off by the idea. I wanted my statement to open the door for a broader understanding of enthusiasm. Some other examples might include, "I'm not the last word on biblical interpretation," or "I'm not the final authority on this," or "I'm not trying to tell you what to do.")

Prayer

O Lord, let Advent be for me a time of spiritual renewal, so that I may come to Christmas with a deeper enthusiasm for serving you with my head, my heart, and my voice. In Jesus' name we pray. Amen.

Focus for the Week

Allow Advent to be a time of considering how you can be a witness to the light that is Jesus, witnessing in ways that are natural, gracious, and likely to be listened to by those who are not already followers of Jesus.

Note: Some parts of this chapter were previously published in Stan Purdum's sermon "Thinking and Feeling Faith" in *Proclaim*, a publication of Parish Publishing, New Canaan, Connecticut.

1 From John 1:24, *Barnes' Notes on the New Testament* (1832). Accessed via QuickVerse Bible program.

2 See the Word History on "enthusiasm," *The American Heritage Dictionary, www.answers.com/topic/enthusiasm*.

3 See the Word History on "enthusiasm," *The American Heritage Dictionary, www.answers.com/topic/enthusiasm*.

4 Quoted in *The Twentieth Century Pulpit*, Volume 2, edited by James W. Cox (Abingdon, 1981); page 90.

5 From "Howard Gotlieb, an Archivist with Persistence, Dies at 79," by Douglas Martin, in *The New York Times*, December 5, 2005, *www.nytimes.com/2005/12/05/national/05gotlieb.html?_r=0*. Accessed July 31, 2013.

General sources consulted for biblical accuracy but not quoted:

New Interpreter's Bible, Volume VIII; page 157.

New Interpreter's Bible, Volume IX; pages 527-528.

The Gospel of John, Volume 1, Revised Edition, The Daily Bible Study Series, by William Barclay (Westminster Press, 1975); pages 76-80.

"Baptism," in *The Dictionary of Bible and Religion*, edited by William H. Gentz (Abingdon, 1986); page 101.

"Sanhedrin," in *The Dictionary of Bible and Religion*, edited by William H. Gentz (Abingdon, 1986); pages 929-930.

Christmas

The Highway
of Merriment

Scripture: Isaiah 62:6-12; Psalm 98; Luke 1:68-79

In the introduction to this study, I said that many worshippers like to skip over Advent hymns and start singing Christmas carols on the Sundays leading up to Christmas. If you're among them, the Highway of Merriment is where you can sing the carols to your heart's content. In fact, I considered calling this chapter "The Highway of Carols," but I didn't want to exclude non-singers, and "merriment" has room for all of us, whether musically inclined or not. If you are a singer, however, feel free to picture yourself now traveling a road toward Christmas singing joyfully. But first, a word about a Christmas song that's not a carol: "Walking in a Winter Wonderland." As a kid, I used to think that one line in it said, "Later on, we'll perspire, as we dream by the fire." I was probably a young teenager before I learned that the word was *conspire*, not *perspire.* (However, long before then, I'd figured out that the "Walking in Our Winter Underwear" version I'd heard some friends sing was not an accurate rendition of the song.)

My perspire/conspire confusion is a *mondegreen*—a term for a word or series of words resulting from the mishearing of a statement or song lyric. It was coined by author Sylvia Wright in a 1954 *Harper's* column in which she admitted to long misunderstanding a sentence in the first stanza of the Scottish ballad, "The Bonny Earl of Murray." That stanza's correct lyrics are:

Ye Highlands and Ye Lowlands,
Oh where hae you been?
They hae slay the Earl of Murray,
And laid him on the green.

But Wright heard the last two lines, as "they hae slay the Earl of Murray, and Lady Mondegreen." Wright titled the column in which she acknowledged her error, "The Death of Lady Mondegreen."[1]

Gavin Edwards has collected a bunch of Christmas mondegreens in his book, *Deck the Halls with Buddy Holly: And Other Misheard Christmas Lyrics.*[2] Here are a few of my favorites from the many Edwards quotes:

Olive, the other reindeer
You'll tell Carol, "Be a skunk, I require" ("Yuletide
    carols being sung by a choir")
On the first day of Christmas, my tulip gave to me

Police have my dad ("Feliz Navidad")
O come, hoggy faithful
Rudolph, the red-nosed reindeer, you'll go drown in
    Listerine
He's making a list, chicken and rice
With the jelly toast proclaim ("With angelic hosts
    proclaim")
Good King Wenceslas looked out on the feet of
    heathens
While shepherds washed their socks at night
Good tidings we bring to you and your kid

Of course, no one can fracture a song better than children, with their limited vocabularies, and it's likely many of these mondegreens originated with them. One lyric children usually get right, however, is "we wish you a merry Christmas!" But when it comes to Christian adults sending Christmas greetings, some are reluctant to use the term "merry." It's not that they don't want to wish others happiness, but they think the phrase "Merry Christmas" suggests an attitude or behavior out of keeping with the religious side of Christmas. Merriment may seem too strongly associated with the secular celebrations and bring to mind images of having too much to drink or of ribald partying.

There's a certain oddness about this reluctance, however, because in recent years, some Christians have launched the so-called "Christmas wars," calling for boycotts of retailers who use "Happy Holidays" or some similar religion-free greeting in their Christmas advertising.

These Christians insist that the stores use "Merry Christmas" instead. Thus, there may be followers of Jesus who boycott stores that don't use "Merry Christmas" in their marketing, and at the same time, search for Christmas cards to send out that use some vocabulary other than *merry*—perhaps "have a blessed Christmas" or "joyous noel" or "glad tidings to you."

Frankly, I don't see how pressuring retailers to use "Merry Christmas" to sell their products honors Jesus, but I also believe that merry is a fine word for the sacred celebration of Christmas. In fact, it's a great word. In my first church appointment, a couple had a baby girl who, practically from the moment of birth, was a cheerful, happy, contented child. So when they named her, they called her Merry Ruth—not M-a-r-y, but M-e-r-r-y. At the time, I thought what a great name it was, and as I apply the word to Christmas, I realize there's plenty about the Incarnation—God coming to us in the birth of Jesus—to make us cheerful, happy, and contented as well.

Christmas Scriptures

What's more, the traditional Scripture readings for Christmas are arranged in a pattern that leads to rejoicing. The Revised Common Lectionary is an official list of recommended Scripture readings for every Sunday and special day of the year on a three-year cycle and is used by preachers in several denominations including United

Methodists. It offers a choice of twelve readings for use
on Christmas Eve/Day. The twelve are divided into three
groupings, called "propers" in lectionary jargon, as follows:

Proper I	**Proper II**	**Proper III**
Isaiah 9:2-7	Isaiah 62:6-12	Isaiah 52:7-10
Titus 2:11-14	Titus 3:4-7	Hebrews 1:1-4,
Luke 2:1-14	Luke 2:(1-7) 8-20	(5-12)
(15-20)	Psalm 97:1-12	John 1:1-14
Psalm 96:1-13		Psalm 98:1-9

In each proper, the Isaiah reading presents an Old
Testament prophecy about the Messiah's arrival. The
Gospel reading tells part of the Christmas story (though
from a theological standpoint in the John passage).
The epistle reading gives a theological perspective on
the coming of Jesus into the world. And all three of the
Psalm readings call for rejoicing. Thus, taken together, the
four readings of each proper 1) report what expectation
Christmas fulfilled and what hope it met, 2) tell what
happened at Christmas, 3) explain what Christmas means,
and 4) call for a merry response. In fact, since the Psalms
were all written to be set to music, we'd be justified in
calling Psalms 96, 97, and 98 *Christmas carols.*

While space here doesn't permit us to examine all
of the texts in these propers, we can look at a couple of
them. Consider first Isaiah 62:6-12. As with the Isaiah 64
passage we discussed in the "Highway of Reversal," this
passage comes from the time when the Jewish exiles had

returned to their homeland and were trying to rebuild their lives. They were finding this to be tough going, and their hope for an era of peace and justice was beginning to fade in the face of great obstacles, including economic hardships, political maneuverings, religious squabbles, security worries, and the daily difficulties of life as a subject people. As biblical commentator Paul D. Hanson explains what was happening,

> The resolve necessary to keep the restoration effort on track was being broken by a crescendo of doubts regarding the credibility of Israel's God. The God who had not prevented the Babylonians and their gods from destroying Jerusalem [seemed] still powerless to reestablish the security of the nation. Or perhaps God was indifferent, lacking in resolve or commitment to this small, struggling community. All of the talk about God coming as Redeemer was mere wishful thinking. A chill was beginning to encircle the hearts of many within the struggling community.[3]

In the midst of that growing gloom, an unnamed prophet speaks of "sentinels" (probably a gathering or "school" of prophets) who are to "call on the LORD. . . / and don't allow God to rest until he establishes Jerusalem, / and makes it the praise of the earth" (verses 6-7). In other words, though the people are back in Jerusalem, it is a wrecked city under domination, and its people are not the light to the nations they were previously envisioned to be (see Isaiah 42:6; 49:6; 60:3). These sentinels see their task as continuing to be on the lookout for the fulfillment of God's promises, and to keep the people faithful and hopeful in waiting for them.

In verse 10, the prophets/sentinels refer to a highway project—building a road and clearing away stones. This echoes the call for a straightened and leveled highway described in Isaiah 40, which we discussed in Chapter 1; but here, the road-clearing call is addressed to people who have already returned home from exile. "But in a metaphorical sense," says Hanson, "they have a long way to go."[4]

Verse 11 looks forward to the day when the sentinels will be able to announce the advent of the Lord: "Look! Your deliverer arrives . . . " And when that happens, says verse 12, the people will be renamed as "The Holy People, Redeemed by the LORD . . . Sought After—A City That Is Not Abandoned."

There is, of course, no mention of merriment here, but the stage is set for it. The gloom of fading hope is the undercurrent of this text, but that means that the day when the deliverer (read "Messiah") comes and the people are redeemed by the LORD will surely be one of rejoicing.

Now, against the backdrop of Isaiah 62, read Psalm 98 with its ecstatic rhapsodizing about the Lord making "his salvation widely known" (Psalm 98:2). At first glance, this would seem an odd pairing, but Psalm 98 is included in a section of the Book of Psalms (Book IV, Psalm 90-106) that one commentator says was "shaped in part to respond to the crisis of exile and its aftermath."[5] So

Psalm 98 could be from the same general time period and from the same community of people as that which produced Isaiah 62.

Psalm 98, along with Psalms 93 and 95-99, are enthronement psalms, songs used by the worshipping community to proclaim God's reign. The psalm begins, calling for worshippers to "Sing to the LORD a new song / because he has done wonderful things!" The people of Israel and Judah knew no shortage of "wonderful things" the Lord had done in their history, with the Exodus being chief among them. But the call for the singing of a *new* song indicates that it's not just a recalling of historical deliverance that's needed. The new song is Psalm 98 itself, which then goes on in verses 1b-3 to summarize the new things God has done: "won the victory," "made his salvation widely known," "revealed his righteousness" to "all the nations," "remembered his loyal love and faithfulness to the house of Israel," and allowed "every corner of the earth" to see "God's salvation." Granted these are general phrases without specifics attached, but they are based on confidence that God reigns and is in charge. In a way, Psalm 98:1-3 is the Old Testament version of "He's Got the Whole World in His Hands."

Then in verses 4-9, the psalmist calls on all the earth to "be happy! Rejoice out loud! Sing [God's] praises!" And not only does the psalmist call all people to rejoice ("the world and all its inhabitants" [verse 7]), but he even calls creation itself to join in the glee:

Let the sea and everything in it roar; . . .
Let all the rivers clap their hands;
   let the mountains rejoice out loud altogether before the LORD
   because he is coming to establish justice on the earth!
(verses 7-9a)

Millennia later, when Isaac Watts was paraphrasing Psalms for use in English churches, he employed 98:4-9 as the basis for his 1719 hymn "Joy to the World," which is certainly one of the most joyous Christmas carols.

The Default Emotion

How can the same community that is facing hardships and has some members who are losing hope also produce joyous psalms? It has to be because some other members of the community—certainly the prophets and probably several others as well—had a larger perspective and were able to draw their hope from what they believed God was yet to do. In other words, they trusted God's promises and believed God reigns, even when evidence of that wasn't obvious. With that mindset, merriment rather than despair is the default emotion.

John Ortberg, who is senior pastor of Menlo Park Presbyterian Church in Menlo Park, California, describes a scenario that helps us understand this. He invites us to imagine that we have a five-year-old daughter who becomes so sick that we fear for her life. But then the doctor tells us that a simple operation will correct the problem, and she will fully recover.

We are not only filled with relief but also with great joy. But our daughter, hearing she must have an operation, is badly frightened, and because she has neither the maturity nor the perspective to look past the immediate situation to the outcome, our telling her that she will be fine doesn't allay her fears. In fact, being lighthearted about her situation makes her think we don't take her fears seriously, and worse, that we don't care. So, to comfort her, we have to remain somber when we're with her so she'll know we empathize.

Nonetheless, when we're not in her hospital room, we can allow our true happy emotions to show, for we know she's going to be fine.[6]

The author of Psalm 98 is something like the parent in that scenario. Yes, he knows about the chill beginning to encircle the hearts of many within the struggling community, but he also knows that in the long run, everything will be all right. And that makes all the difference.

After describing the sick-daughter scenario, Ortberg points to Revelation 21:3-4: "God himself will be with them as their God. He will wipe away every tear from their eyes. Death will be no more. There will be no mourning, crying, or pain anymore, for the former things have passed away." God knows that these verses describe the way things are going to be, Ortberg says, but with us, God is like the parent of the sick child. He has to take our anxiety seriously, but every so often, he goes outside and laughs, because he knows everything will be all right in the end.

Ortberg then directs us to the words G.K. Chesterton, a noted Christian writer of the early twentieth century, used to conclude his book, *Orthodoxy*. Chesterton said that though Jesus let his grief, sadness, and anger show on his face, he had to restrain himself from smiling because he knew Christianity's great secret—that the promise of God's kingdom is *true*. Like the parent in Ortberg's story, Jesus had to restrain himself from breaking out in joy in order to meet us where we are in our worries and our fears, but joy was his "default emotion." Chesterton didn't use that term, but he said this: "There was some one thing that was too great for God to show us when He walked upon our earth; and I have sometimes fancied that it was His mirth."[7]

Another Christmas Carol

I've suggested that the Psalms the church designates for Christmas could be called Christmas carols, but there's also at least one song from the Gospels that can be included in that category as well. It's found in Luke 1:68-79, and the church calls it the *Benedictus*, after its first word in the Latin translation. The lyrics come from Zechariah, the father of John the Baptist. He sang them after John was born to him and his wife Elizabeth in their old age. An angel had informed Zechariah in advance of the special mission his son would have (Luke 1:11-17), and so now the old man has not only the joy that comes to most fathers when their child is born but also the pleasure of knowing that his child will play a role in the redemption of his people.

We don't know what tune Zechariah used—possibly it was a chant of some sort—but the lyrics get at the heart of Christmas. Jesus was still in his mother's womb at this point, but from the angel, Zechariah had understood that the birth of *his* child, John, was to be a primary link in a chain of events that would culminate in the salvation of the world.

The words of his song are in poetic format, but look at what they say: God has

come to help and deliver his people;

raised up a mighty savior for us;

brought us salvation from our enemies;

shown us the mercy promised to our ancestors;

remembered his holy covenant with us;

enabled us to serve him without fear, while being judged holy and righteous;

told us how to be saved through the forgiveness of our sins;

given light to us who are sitting in darkness and in the
shadow of death, to guide us on the path of peace.

In the song, Zechariah also addresses his newborn son,
predicting that people will call him "a prophet of the Most
High" (verse 76) because he will be the forerunner for the
Savior, announcing deliverance.

This song is filled with themes that have deep
significance for people whose lives are not going the way
they want them to—that is to say, most of us at least
some of the time. Those themes are redemption, mercy,
deliverance, freedom from fear (assurance), salvation,
forgiveness, and peace, and we could make a lesson on
any one of them.

Instead of doing that, however, consider them together
as representative of the action of God in the lives of those
who trust him. One way to do that is to picture a balance
scale. On the one side, pile up all the stuff that weighs
down on us, that sucks the joy and meaning out of life.
There we would place disappointment, fear, pain, loss,
grief, shame, trouble, hurt, conflict, bad news, and similar
kinds of realities.

Now picture the other side of the scale, and think
about what happens as God loads it. He piles on, one
after another, redemption, mercy, deliverance, assurance,
salvation, forgiveness, and peace. Which side is heavier?
Which side moves our lives more?

There are certainly times when all we can feel is the
pain and trouble side, when it feels like the weight of the

world is on our shoulders, pressing us down, grinding us away, knocking the breath out of us, and causing our legs to give way under us. In fact, that's a reasonable description of the Jewish people of Zechariah's day, living as they did as a subjugated people under the heavy thumb of Rome and ruled directly by the crazed vassal-king Herod, a man who stomped anybody who got in his way.

But in the midst of that, Zechariah learned that the birth of his son John was calling attention to what God was doing on the *other side* of the scale of life, putting God's good gifts there. And although Zechariah probably did not have the scale metaphor in mind, he was, in effect, saying that redemption weighs more than loss, forgiveness weighs more than guilt, assurance weighs more than fear, deliverance weighs more than oppression, and so on.

Ironically, the greater weight of God's good gifts does not increase our load. That's because when we are under the life-killing side of the scale, the growing weight of all that God puts on the other side *lifts* the tonnage of hurt and despair that has been bearing down on us. Perhaps that's why, in another Gospel, Jesus said, "Come to me, all you who are struggling hard and carrying heavy loads, and I will give you rest." And then he added, "My burden is light" (Matthew 11:28, 30).

The event set in motion with the birth of John the Baptist, of course, took another step forward with the birth of Jesus. This is what makes Zechariah's song Christmas music. The Incarnation of God in the Baby of Bethlehem means that God put himself in a place to feel the crushing weight of the trouble side of the scale. As a human being, Jesus was subject to the same difficult realities all of us are, and frankly, he got a wallop of them; in fact, they took his life. Christmas thus tells us that God came in Jesus to hurt *with* us. Therefore, he knows why we need to have the weight of trouble, grief, and hurt lifted by offsetting it with redemption, mercy, deliverance, assurance, salvation, forgiveness, and peace.

New father Zechariah sang not only about his own son but also about the Son of God for whom John was to be a forerunner. Thus, Zechariah's song is *real* Christmas music.

Merry Christmas

I mentioned Christmas lyrics that kids misunderstand. There's one lyric that grownups often hear incorrectly as well. Here's the title with the comma omitted: "God Rest Ye Merry Gentlemen." So where does the comma belong? Most people sing it as though it comes after "ye": God Rest Ye, Merry Gentlemen. But it isn't written that way. It comes after "merry": God Rest Ye Merry, Gentlemen. (By the way, one mondegreen for this carol is, "Get dressed you married gentlemen!"[8])

That comma really is the difference between a Christian Christmas and a secular one. To say "merry gentlemen" suggests that we have manufactured our merriment. It may have even come from drinking too much eggnog. But the other way, with its strange Old English, is saying "God rest ye with the merriment *God* gives." Thus, "Merry Christmas" invites us to celebrate the joyful good news that's true no matter how up or down we feel personally—the merriment that Christ has come into the world, the merriment that is anything but contrived and is not dependent on our current situation.

Christmas isn't about superficial or momentary fun, but about the deep-down merriment that comes from God, the awareness that we are part of something bigger than ourselves and the confidence that our lives are in the hands of a personal God who can be trusted to bring about the ultimate best for us.

So, Merry Christmas!

Questions for Reflection and Discussion

1. Have you been reluctant to use "merry" in your Christmas greetings to others? Why or why not?

2. When have you felt like the returned exiles described in the Paul D. Hanson quote above? What, if anything, helped you regain confidence in God?

3. In what ways do you draw hope from what you believe God has *yet* to do?

4. What do you make of Chesterton's suggestion that Christ's default emotion is mirth? How might this help you in your daily life?

5. Comment on this: "Merry Christmas" invites us to celebrate the joyful good news that is true no matter how up or down we feel personally—the merriment that Christ has come into the world, the merriment that is anything but contrived and is not dependent on our current situation. Is there a deeply rooted joy in your life?

Prayer

Thank you for the merriment of Christmas, O Lord. Plant it deep in my soul, so that even when the weight of the world is on my shoulders, the rhythm of your joy will sustain me. In Jesus' name we pray. Amen.

Focus for the Week

You'll likely be singing or at least hearing some Christmas carols this week. Enjoy them, but if you have a few moments for reflection, consider what the lyrics are actually saying.

1 From *Have Yourself a Punny Little Christmas: Word Play for the Holidays,* by Richard Lederer (Wyrick & Company, 2006); page 51.

2 From *Deck the Halls with Buddy Holly: And Other Misheard Christmas Lyrics,* by Gavin Edwards (Harper Perennial, 1998).

3 From *Isaiah 40-66, Interpretation: A Bible Commentary for Teaching and Preaching,* by Paul D. Hanson (John Knox Press, 1995); page 227.

4 From *Isaiah 40-66;* page 229.

5 From *The New Interpreter's Bible*, Volume IV, by J. Clinton McCann, Jr. (Abingdon, 1996); page 1072.

6 From "Hunger for Joy," by John Ortberg in *Christian Century*, September 4, 2007; page 39.

7 From *Orthodoxy* (Image Books, 1991; Reprint of 1908 book from Dodd, Mead & Co.); page 170. Also quoted in the Ortberg article.

8 From *www.snopes.com/holidays/christmas/humor/ mondegreens.asp*.

General sources consulted for biblical accuracy but not quoted:

"The Book of Isaiah 40-66," *New Interpreter's Bible*, Volume VI; pages 309-323.

"Isaiah 62:6-12," *The Lectionary Commentary: The First Readings* (William B. Eerdmans, 2001), 388-392.

"Hymn or Song of Praise," in *New Interpreter's Bible*, Volume IV; pages 648-649.

The Interpreter's Bible, Volume 4 (Abingdon, 1955); pages 518-520.

New Interpreter's Bible, Volume IX; pages 58-61.